Alfred's Premier Piano Course

Dennis Alexander • Gayle Kowalchyk • E. L. Lancaster • Victoria McArthur • Martha Mier

Edited by Morton Manus

Cover Design by Ted Engelbart
Interior Design by Tom Gerou
Illustrations by Jimmy Holder
Music Engraving by Linda Lusk

Contents

A Note to Teachers. 2
A Note to Students (and Parents) 3
How to Sit at the Piano 4
The Secret to a Good Hand Position. 5
Notes
Quarter Note. 6
The Keyboard: Two Black Keys. 7
Rests
Quarter Rest 8
The Keyboard: Three Black Keys 10
Bar Lines and Measures 11
Half Note 12
Dynamic Signs (f and p) 13
Whole Note. 15
Time Signature ($\frac{4}{4}$). 16
Damper Pedal 17
The Music Alphabet 18
Keyboard Anchor: D 19
Dynamic Sign (mf) 20
Keyboard Anchors: G and A 22
Whole Rest 24
Step. 26
New Time Signature ($\frac{3}{4}$)
Dotted Half Note. 28
The Staff 32

Bass Clef
Treble Clef 33
Reading Middle C
The Grand Staff 34
Half Rest 35
Bass F 36
Tempo 37
Whole Rest in $\frac{3}{4}$ 38
Treble G. 39
Landmark Notes. 41
New Note G (Bass) 42
New Note E (Bass). 43
New Landmark Note: Bass C 44
New Note D (Bass) 45
Stepping Up from Bass C 46
New Notes D and E (Treble) 48
New Note F (Treble) 49
Stepping Up from Middle C 50
New Notes B and A (Bass) 53
Stepping Down from Middle C. 54
Skip 56
Skip Up from Middle C 57
Skip Up from D (Treble) 58
Skip Down from B (Bass) 61

A Note to Teachers

Welcome to *Alfred's Premier Piano Course*, a student-, parent- and teacher-friendly approach to piano lessons!

Lesson Book 1A is available in the two versions: Book with CD (#20652) and Book without CD (#22356).

The books and CDs (described on pages 3 and 65) provide a fully integrated and comprehensive approach to piano instruction.

The following overview outlines four important areas from the course's distinctive and imaginative approach.

Note Reading

- Notes in bass clef are introduced first, to prevent students from becoming weaker bass-clef readers.

- Instead of relying on fixed hand positions, students learn to recognize important landmark notes.

- Intervals are introduced sequentially and reinforced creatively.

- Many Lesson Book pages include *Sight-Reading* exercises for reinforcement.

- Use of varied fingerings prevents students from relating specific notes to finger numbers.

Rhythm Reading

- Rhythms are read in multiple-note patterns rather than as single notes.

- Playing with a steady pulse is emphasized.

- Rhythmic, musical duets support and enhance student performance.

- Eighth notes, often a stumbling block among beginners, are delayed until Lesson Book 2A.

Technical Development

- Technique is developed equally in both hands.

- Short, effective technical exercises called *Workouts* are included where needed.

- Students learn to move effectively to explore the entire range of the keyboard.

Creative Thinking and Musicality

- Duet accompaniments introduce a variety of musical styles and encourage stylistic performance.

- A *Closer Look* provides helpful hints to aid the learning process.

- Performance skills and musical understanding are enhanced through *Premier Performer* suggestions.

- Many pages include *Imagination Stations* to engage the student in expansive, creative activities.

A Note to Students (and Parents)

You are about to begin an exciting musical journey that will teach you to play the piano. The best part is that you won't be traveling alone. You'll be joined by your teacher and parents. *Alfred's Premier Piano Course* will lead the way.

Let's begin by exploring your books:

Lesson Book

- Available in two versions: with CD (#20652) or without CD (#22356).
- Learn about music by taking a *Closer Look*.
- Become a *Premier Performer* by playing more than notes and rhythm.
- Discover facts about important composers.
- Listen to the music on the CD (if included) or General MIDI disk (available separately #23258) and play along to make learning fun. See information about the CD on page 65.

Theory Book

- *Fun Zone*—Play written games and solve puzzles.
- *Imagination Station*— Learn to compose and create.
- *Now Hear This*—Learn how to listen to music through ear training.
- *Now Play This*—Learn to sight-read music.
- *Learning Links*— Discover facts related to history, science and interesting subjects from daily life based on the music and activities in the course.

At-Home Book

- Organize your practice time by following your teacher's instructions on the convenient Assignment Pages.
- Read P. J. and Sara's amazing story about playing the piano while traveling around the world with the incredible *Music Imagination Machine*.
- Share music and practice time with parents.

Performance Book

- A CD is included with the book.
- Play additional pieces for friends and family.
- Listen to the music on the CD or General MIDI disk (available separately #23258) and play along.

Flash Cards

- *Music Cards*—Review important information from the *Lesson Book*.
- *Sight-Reading Cards*— Practice sight-reading at the keyboard.

Just turn the page to start your journey. Meet new people, discover new places and begin an exciting adventure you'll never forget.

How to Sit at the Piano

Start with these checklists each time you play to make sure you are sitting correctly at the piano.

Check the Height of the Bench

✔ Your feet are flat on the floor, right foot slightly forward. (If your feet do not touch the floor, use a foot stool.)

✔ When your hands are on the keys, your elbows and arms are level with the keyboard. (If they are not, sit on a book or cushion.)

Check Your Distance from the Keyboard

✔ Sit on the front half of the bench, and lean slightly forward.

✔ Extend your arms straight ahead, with your hands loosely cupped and elbows slightly bent.

✔ Adjust the bench forward or backward so that your knuckles touch the open keyboard cover.

Check Your Posture

✔ Sit tall, with relaxed shoulders.

✔ Your upper arms hang loosely from your shoulders.

Closer Look

Help your teacher sit correctly at the keyboard.

Teacher: *Demonstrate items from the checklists incorrectly. Ask the student to identify what is wrong.*

The Secret to a Good Hand Position

Find a Good Hand Position

✔ Stand up straight with your arms hanging loosely

by your sides and your hands in a relaxed position.

✔ Keep your hands in the same relaxed position

as you sit at the piano.

✔ Now place your hands on the keyboard.

Check Your Hands

✔ Your hands are slightly curved and relaxed.

✔ Each hand is shaped like it is gently holding a bubble.

✔ Always play on the side tip of the thumb

and the fingertip pads of the other fingers.

Finger Numbers

*For playing the piano,
each finger is given a number.
Memorize them.*

LH
(left hand)

RH
(right hand)

Workout 1 Finger Greetings

● Place your hands together, with fingertips touching.

● Steadily tap together:

→ Both finger 1's.

→ Both finger 2's.

→ Both finger 3's.

→ Both finger 4's.

→ Both finger 5's.

● Place both hands on a table top or closed
keyboard cover and tap matching numbered fingers.

Notes

Notes tell how long sounds last.

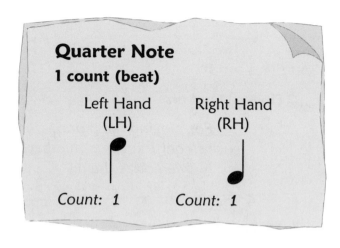

Quarter Note

1 count (beat)

Left Hand (LH)	Right Hand (RH)
Count: 1	Count: 1

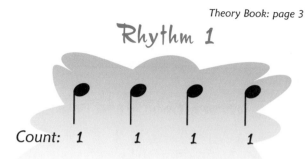

Theory Book: page 3

Rhythm 1

Count: 1   1   1   1

Your teacher may suggest another way to count.

1. Just like you, music has a heartbeat called **pulse**. Using *both hands*, tap a steady pulse on your lap as your teacher plays the duet below.

2. On the closed keyboard cover, tap Rhythm 1, first with your LH, then with your RH, as you count aloud. Repeat several times. *Reminder:* Keep a steady pulse.

3. Tap *Steady Quarter Notes* (below) evenly on your lap as your teacher plays the duet part.

Steady Quarter Notes

Begin with your LH.

RH

LH

Tap on your lap.

RH

LH

Tap again from the beginning.

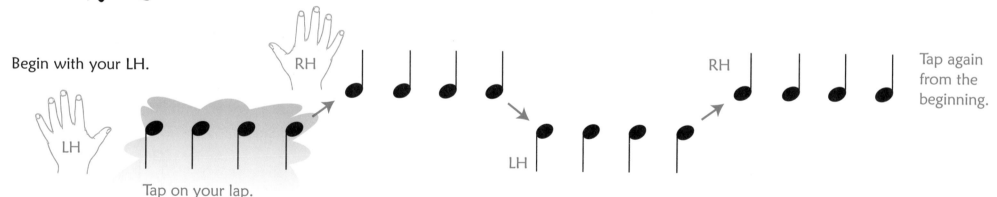

Moderate and steady, without swing

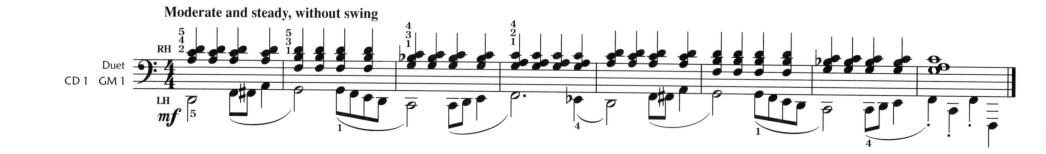

Duet
CD 1   GM 1

The Keyboard: Two Black Keys

The piano keyboard has black keys and white keys. The black keys are in groups of 2's and 3's.

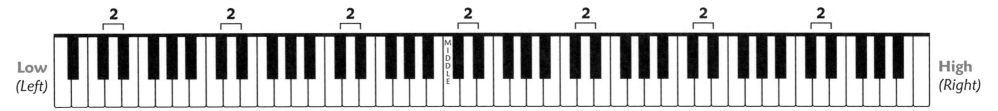

Low
(Left)

High
(Right)

1. Use LH fingers 3–2 together to play all the 2-black-key groups from *low* to *high*.

2. Use RH fingers 2–3 together to play all the 2-black-key groups from *high* to *low*.

Hand Position

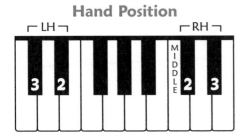

┌ LH ┐   ┌ RH ┐

3 2   2 3

Our Journey

Play moderately (medium) loud.

Play again.

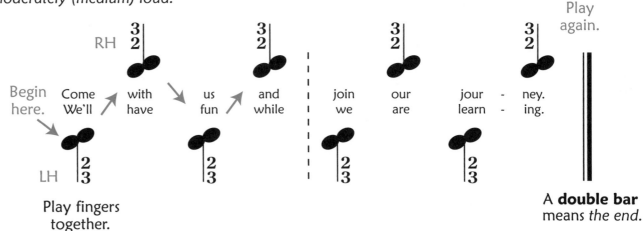

Practice Journal *(for pages 7–11)*

✔ Tap the rhythm on your lap with the correct fingers and count aloud.

✔ Play as you say the words aloud.

RH

Begin here.

| Come | with | us | and | | join | our | jour | - | ney. |
| We'll | have | fun | while | | we | are | learn | - | ing. |

LH

Play fingers together.

A **double bar** means *the end.*

Adapted from *Peter, Peter, Pumpkin Eater*

Happily

RH 2   RH over   1.   RH over   2.

Duet
CD 2/3 GM 2

mf LH 2

Theory Book: page 5

Rests

Rests are signs of silence.

Quarter Rest
1 count (beat)

Count: rest

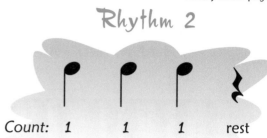

Count: *1   1   1   rest*

Your teacher may suggest another way to count.

Tap and count aloud 3 times each day.

In *Treasure Map*,
notes step down  or repeat

Treasure Map

LH
MIDDLE **3 2**

Play moderately loud.

Dig - ging down,

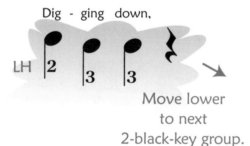

LH 2   3   3

**Move lower
to next
2-black-key group.**

nev - er   stop,

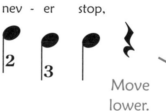

2   3

**Move
lower.**

where the   X

2   3

**Move
lower.**

marks the   spot!

2   3

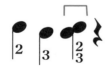

Premier Performer

Play Treasure Map *again,
using this pattern:*

2   3   2
          3

Slow march

8va - - - - - - - - -

Duet
CD 4/5 GM 3

RH 2   3
        1

mp LH 2   LH 2   2

LH 2   LH 2

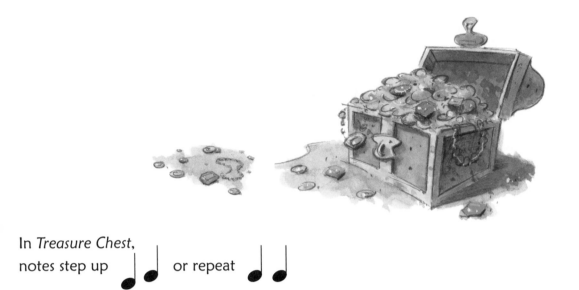

Workout 2 Piano Hands

- Lay your RH flat on the closed keyboard cover.

- Gently slide your fingertips toward your palm until your hand is in a rounded position, like holding a bubble.

- Your wrist should gently be raised so it is level with the back of the hand.

- Repeat with the LH.

In *Treasure Chest,*
notes step up or repeat

Treasure Chest

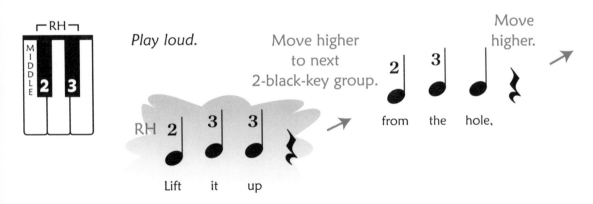

Play loud.

Move higher to next 2-black-key group.

Lift it up

from the hole,

Move higher.

treas - ure chest

Move higher.

filled with gold.

Premier Performer

Play Treasure Chest again, using this pattern:

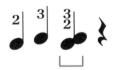

Duet
CD 6/7 GM 4

With confidence

Theory Book: page 7

The Keyboard: Three Black Keys

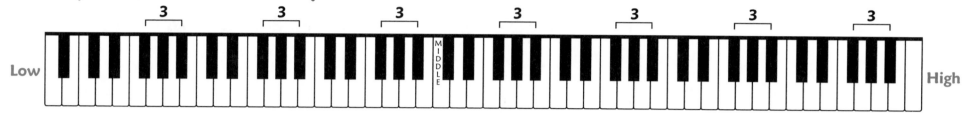

Low   **High**

1. Use LH fingers 4–3–2 together to play all the 3-black-key groups from *low* to *high*.

2. Use RH fingers 2–3–4 together to play all the 3-black-key groups from *high* to *low*.

Practice Carefully

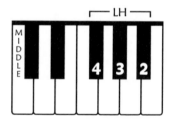

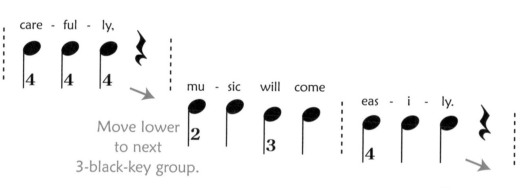

Play soft.

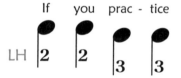

Move lower to next 3-black-key group.

Play two more times.
Move lower each time.

Slowly and gently

Duet
CD 8/9 GM 5

pp

Bar Lines and Measures

Bar lines divide music into equal **measures.**

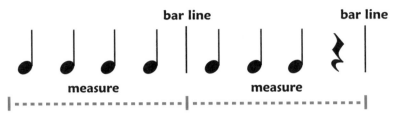

bar line   bar line

measure   measure

Workout 3 Develop Strong Joints

- On a tabletop, place your LH in a rounded playing position.

- While keeping each joint firm, gently press the joint closest to the nail of each LH finger with RH finger 2. Resist the gentle pressure from the RH.

- Repeat, reversing hands.

It's Fun to Play!

THURSDAY   FRIDAY   SATURDAY

Play two more times.
Move higher each time.

Play loud.

Move higher
to next
3-black-key group.

RH **2** **2** **3** **3** | **4** **4** **4**

When you prac - tice | ev - 'ry day,

2 | **3**

you will find it's

4

fun to play!

Imagination Station

*The duet on page 7 is played on the black keys.
Your teacher will show you how to play it.*

Moderately fast

Duet
CD 10/11 GM 6

Half Note

2 counts (beats)

1 half note = 2 quarter notes

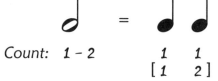

Count: *1 - 2*   *1*   *1*
                   [*1*   *2*]

LH   RH

Taking Turns

Play moderately loud.

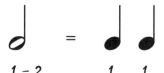

LH |**4** |**3** |**2**

First   it's   your   turn,
When   we   take   turns,

Rhythm 3

Count: *1 - 2*   *1 - 2*

Your teacher may suggest another way to count.

Tap and count aloud 3 times each day.

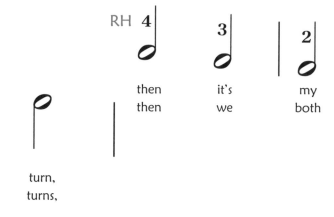

RH |**4** |**3** |**2** |

then   it's   my   turn.
then   we   both   learn.

Practice Journal *(for pages 12–18)*

Keep your eyes on the music.

✔ Tap the rhythm on your lap with the correct hand and count aloud.
✔ Play the piece on the closed keyboard cover as you say the finger numbers aloud.
✔ Play and count aloud.
✔ Play and sing (or say) the words aloud.

Repeat Sign

:|| ← Two dots mean go back to the beginning and play again.

Imagination Station

Play Our Journey *on page 7, changing quarter notes (♩) to half notes (𝅗𝅥).*

Moderately fast
Both hands 8va

Duet
CD 12/13 GM 7

mp

Dynamic Signs

Dynamic signs add variety to music
by telling how *loud* or *soft* to play.

f *(forte)*
means *loud*.

p *(piano)*
means *soft*.

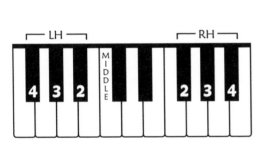

Rhythm 4

Count: 1 – 2   1   1

Your teacher may suggest another way to count.

Tap and count aloud 3 times each day.

Great News

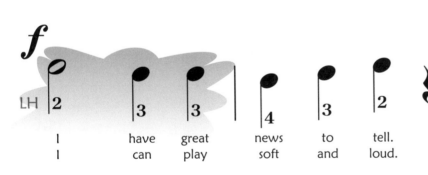

f

LH **2** I I
3 have / can
3 great / play
4 news / soft
3 to / and
2 tell. / loud.

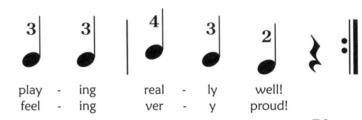

RH **2** I'm / I'm
3 play / feel
3 ing / ing
4 real / ver
3 ly / y
2 well! / proud! 𝄽

***Play p
2nd time***

Duet: Student plays one octave higher.

CD 14/15 GM 8

Workout 4 **Sitting Tall**

- Slump over, with your head and shoulders completely relaxed.

- Imagine a string attached from the top of your head to the ceiling.

- Pretend you are gradually pulled up, until you are sitting tall and relaxed at the piano.

Rhythm 5

Count: 1   1   1 - 2

Your teacher may suggest another way to count.

Tap and count aloud 3 times each day.

Dream Big Dreams

When you're young you dream big dreams, plan big plans, scheme big schemes.

RH **2 3 2 3**   **2**   **3**   **4**

f means _____

Go to next line and play with LH.

Measure number

5 Be- ing young is lots of fun— you can ask an - y - one.

LH **2 3 2 3**   **2**   **3**   **4**

p means _____

Play again with both hands:
1. very low
2. very high

✦ *Premier Performer*   *Play both lines of Dream Big Dreams at the same time, hands together. Play both hands **moderately loud**.*

Duet: Student plays one octave higher.

Flowing

CD 16/17   GM 9

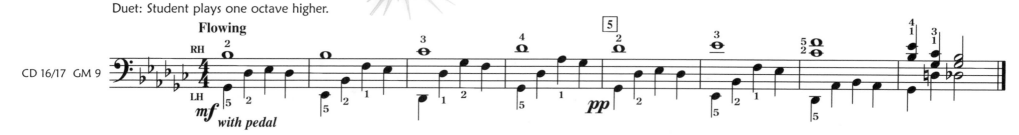

mf *with pedal*   *pp*

Whole Note

4 counts (beats)

Theory Book: page 13

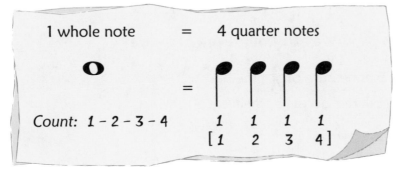

1 whole note	=	4 quarter notes

Count: 1 – 2 – 3 – 4   1 1 1 1
                         [1 2 3 4]

Rhythm 6

Count: 1   1   1   1   1 – 2 – 3 – 4

Your teacher may suggest another way to count.

Tap and count aloud 3 times each day.

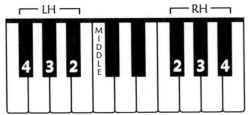

Merrily We Roll Along

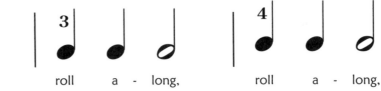

RH 𝒇 Mer – ri – ly   we   roll   a – long,   roll   a – long,   roll   a – long,

Go to next line and play with LH.

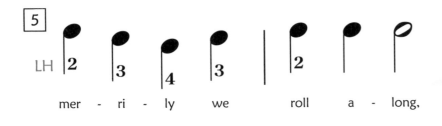

LH mer – ri – ly   we   roll   a – long,   on   our   way   to   school!

Duet: Student plays one octave higher.

With bounce

CD 18/19 GM 10

Time Signature

Two numbers at the beginning of every piece.

$\frac{4}{4}$ means 4 counts in every measure.

$\frac{4}{4}$ means a quarter note ♩ gets 1 count.

Theory Book: page 14
Performance Book: page 5

A New Way to Count—by Measure

Each measure of $\frac{4}{4}$ time has
4 quarter notes (or their equal).

$\frac{4}{4}$ ♩ ♩ ♩ ♩ | o ‖

Count: 1   2   3   4   1 – 2 – 3 – 4

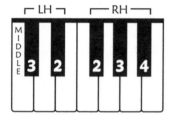

Old MacDonald Had a Dog

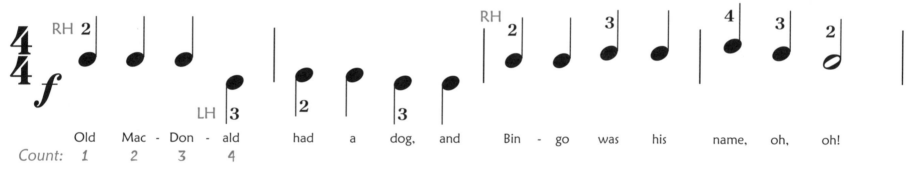

Old Mac - Don - ald   had   a   dog, and   Bin - go   was   his   name, oh,   oh!

Count: 1   2   3   4

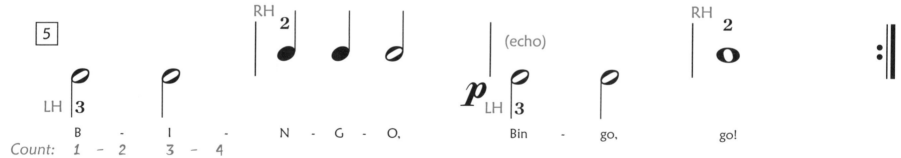

B -   I -   N - G - O,   (echo)   Bin - go,   go!

Count: 1 - 2   3 - 4

Duet: Student plays one octave higher.

With energy

CD 20/21 GM 11

Damper Pedal

Pianos have either 2 or 3 pedals.
The pedal on the right is the **damper pedal.**

When the damper pedal is pressed down, tones last longer.

● Use your right foot

● Heel on the floor

● Ankle relaxed

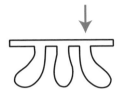 **Writing Time**

1. Circle the time signature and tell your teacher what it means.

2. Finish writing the counts under the measures.

$\frac{4}{4}$ ♩ ♩ ♩ | ♩ ♩ ♩ ♩ | o |

　　　 1　2　3 – 4

Fortune Cookies

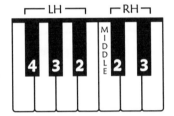

Press the damper pedal and hold throughout.

Won - ton soup,   lots of rice,   or - ange chick - en   would be nice.

Count: 1　2　3 – 4   1　2　3 – 4

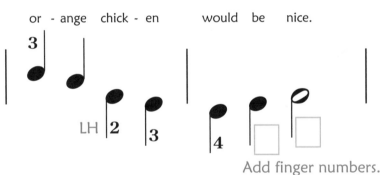

Add finger numbers.

What's the best   part of all?   For - tune cook - ies   for us all.

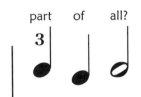

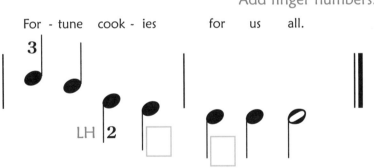

Delicately
Both hands 8va

Duet
CD 22/23 GM 12

18

Theory Book: page 16

The Music Alphabet

The white keys on the piano are named using the first 7 letters of the alphabet. These names repeat over and over.

Middle

Low | High

A B C D E F G (repeating)

Name and play every white key on the keyboard, beginning at the low end and moving up.
Use LH 3 for keys below Middle C and use RH 3 for Middle C and above.

Climbing the Music Ladder

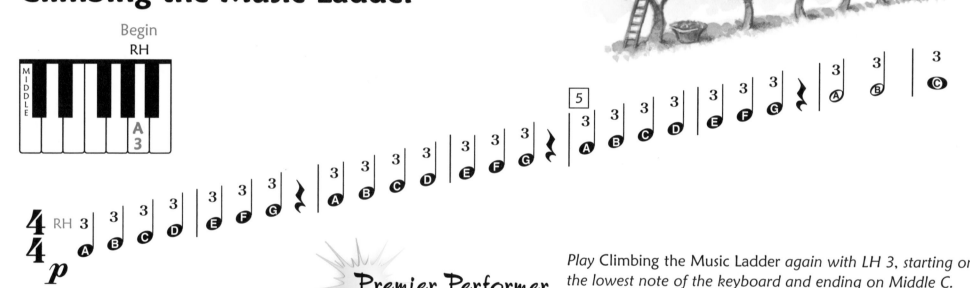

Premier Performer

Play Climbing the Music Ladder *again with LH 3, starting on the lowest note of the keyboard and ending on Middle C.*

Teacher: *Do not play the duet with Premier Performer.*

Duet
CD 24/25 GM 13

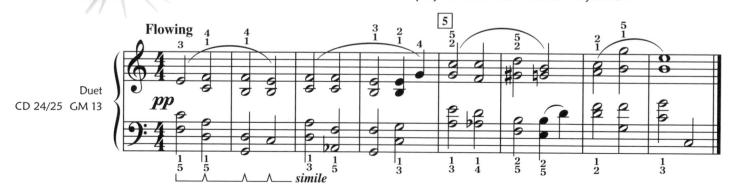

Keyboard Anchor: D

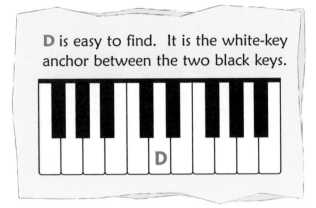

D is easy to find. It is the white-key anchor between the two black keys.

D

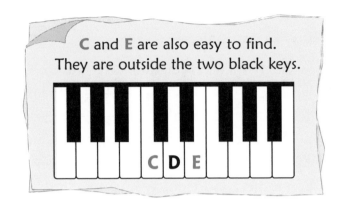

C and **E** are also easy to find. They are outside the two black keys.

C **D** **E**

1. Write the music alphabet three times.   A _____

2. Begin in the middle of the keyboard and:
- play all the D's going *higher* with RH 2.
- play all the D's going *lower* with LH 2.

3. Begin in the middle of the keyboard and:
- play all the C's going *higher* with RH 3.
- play all the E's going *lower* with LH 3.

4. On the keyboard:

- write a **D** on all the D's.
- write a **C** on all the C's.
- write an **E** on all the E's.

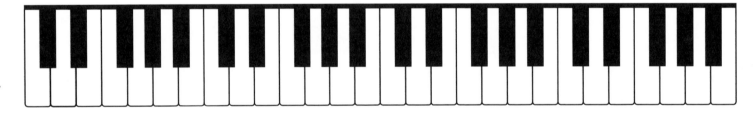

5. Play the following rhythms in the middle of the piano. Count aloud.

- RH 2 on **C**

- RH 3 on **E**

- RH 1 on **D**

- Play the above rhythms again with LH.

Dynamic Sign

mf **(mezzo forte)**

means *moderately (medium) loud*
(softer than *f* and louder than *p*)

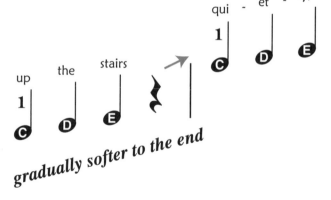

Practice Journal *(for pages 20–43)*

✔ Tap the rhythm and count aloud by measure.
✔ Play the piece on the closed keyboard cover as you say the finger numbers aloud.
✔ Play on the piano as you sing (or say) the note names.
✔ Play and count aloud.
✔ Play and sing (or say) the words aloud.

Up the Attic Stairs

Tell your teacher what 4/4 means.

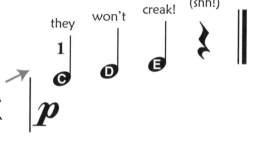

gradually softer to the end

4/4 RH 1

mf

If C we D sneak E

up 1 C the D stairs E

qui- 1 C et- D ly, E

p

they 1 C won't D creak! E (shh!)

Premier Performer

Play Up the Attic Stairs *again, beginning with LH 4–3–2, followed by RH 2–3–4. Alternate hands as you* **move up.**

Duet
CD 26/27 GM 14

Sneakily

mp   *dim.*   *pp*

LH

MIDDLE
C 3
D 2
E 1

Down the Attic Stairs

$\frac{4}{4}$ LH *mf*

What's E 1
that D 2
sound? C 3

We E 1
are D
scared! C

gradually louder to the end

Let's E 1
go D
back C

down E 1
those D
stairs! C

f

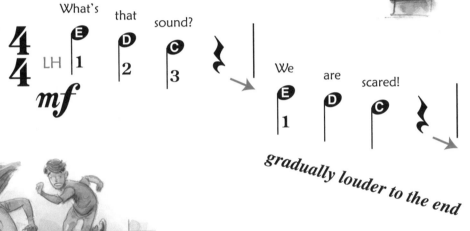

Premier Performer *Play* Down the Attic Stairs *again, beginning with RH 4–3–2, followed by LH 2–3–4. Alternate hands as you* **move down.**

Duet
CD 28/29 GM 15

Moderately

Theory Book: page 18
Performance Book: pages 8–9

Keyboard Anchors: G and A

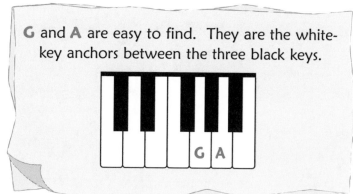

G and A are easy to find. They are the white-key anchors between the three black keys.

Begin in the middle of the keyboard and:

- play all the G's going *lower* with LH 3.

- play all the A's going *higher* with RH 3.

Old MacDonald Had a Mouse

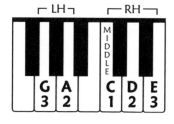

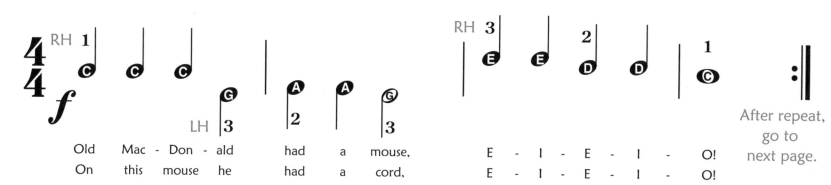

Old Mac - Don - ald had a mouse,   E - I - E - I - O!
On this mouse he had a cord,   E - I - E - I - O!

After repeat,
go to
next page.

Duet: Student plays one octave higher.

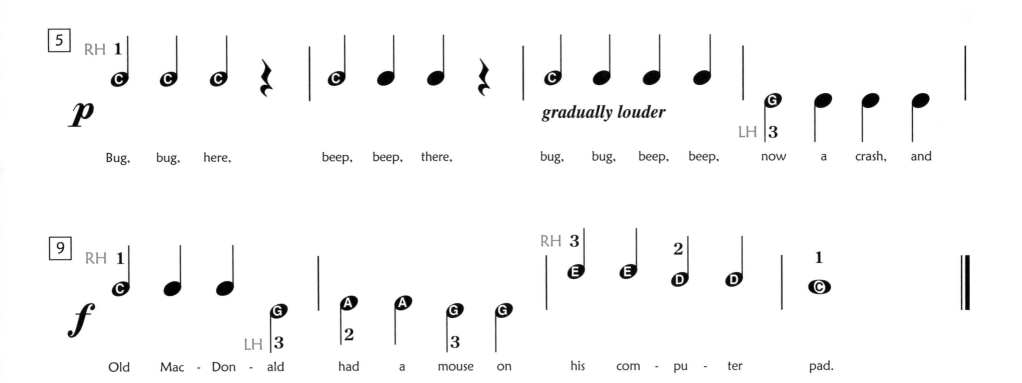

Closer Look *Repeated notes have the same name.*
Circle each group of two or more repeated notes
in Old MacDonald.

Whole Rest

Rest for a whole measure.

In $\frac{4}{4}$ time, the whole rest gets
4 counts (beats) of silence.

1 whole rest　　　=　　4 quarter rests

▬　　=　　𝄽 𝄽 𝄽 𝄽

Count:　1 – 2 – 3 – 4　　　1　2　3　4
　or:　Rest – 2 – 3 – 4　　Rest Rest Rest Rest

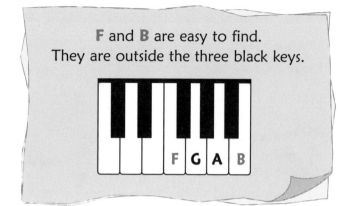

F and **B** are easy to find.
They are outside the three black keys.

Begin in the middle of the keyboard and:

- play all the F's going *higher* with RH 2.
- play all the B's going *lower* with LH 3.

Rock Wall

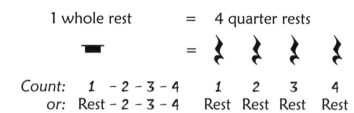

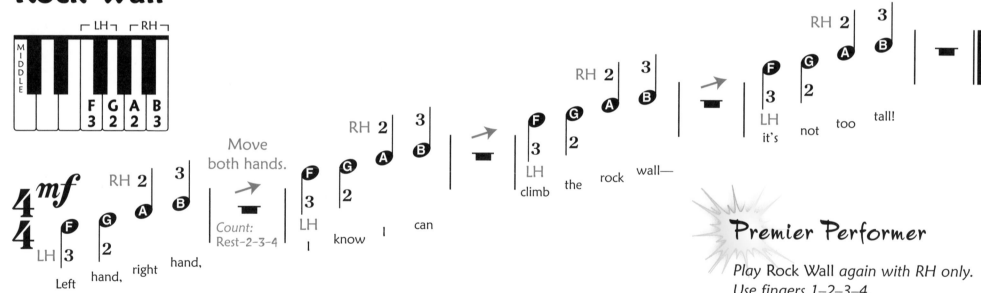

Premier Performer

Play Rock Wall *again with RH only.
Use fingers 1–2–3–4.*

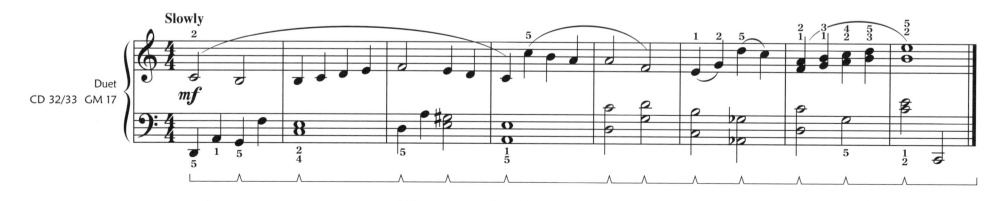

Slowly

Duet
CD 32/33 GM 17

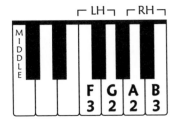

Climbing Down

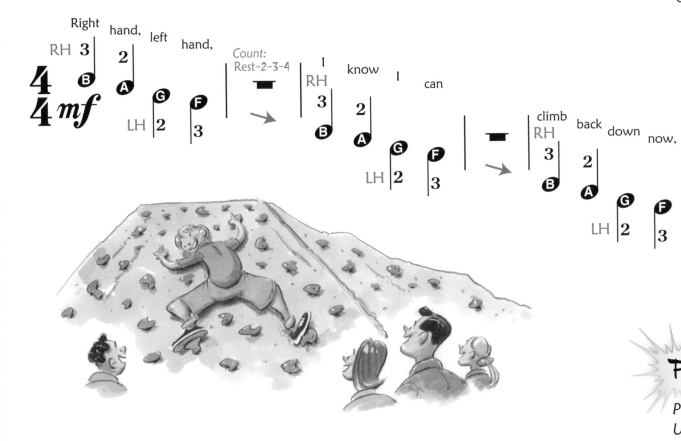

Right hand, left hand,

Count: Rest–2–3–4 I know I can climb back down now, 'cause I know how!

Workout 5 Silent Touch

● Use each rest in *Rock Wall* and *Climbing Down* to move your hands to the new position.

● Silently practice each piece (touch, but do not press the keys) 3 times a day to become an expert at moving up and down the keyboard.

Premier Performer

Play Climbing Down *again with LH only. Use fingers 1–2–3–4.*

Duet
CD 34/35
GM 18

Performance Book: page 10

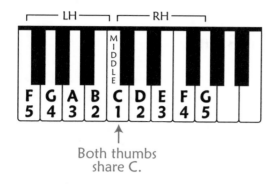

Both thumbs
share C.

Step

A step moves up or down to the:

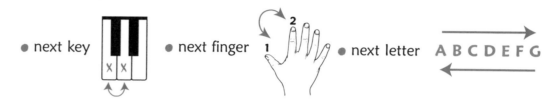

- next key   - next finger   - next letter   A B C D E F G

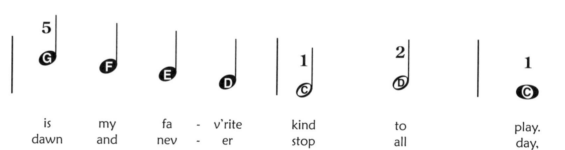

A Jazzy Tune

Say the note names aloud as you play.

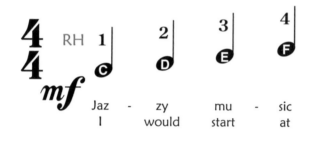

Jaz	zy	mu	sic		is	my	fa	v'rite	kind	to	play.
I	would	start	at		dawn	and	nev	er	stop	all	day,

5

I	would	like	to		play	a	jaz	zy	tune	each	day!
take	a	break,	then		play	all	night	and	swing	and	sway.

Play p
2nd time

Duet: Student plays one octave higher.

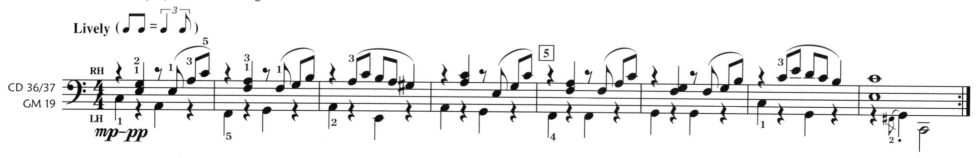

CD 36/37
GM 19

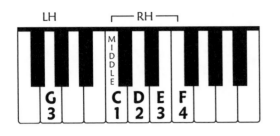

Hush, Little Baby

Writing Time

Draw a line through the noteheads for the RH of *Hush, Little Baby*.

- For repeated notes, the line is straight (horizontal):

- For notes that step, the line slants slightly up or down:

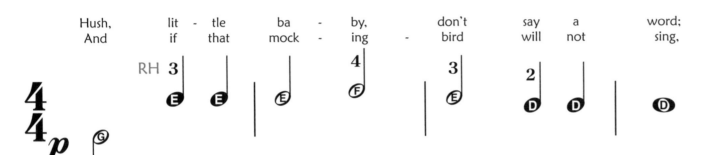

Hush,   lit - tle   ba - by,   don't   say   a   word;
And   if   that   mock - ing - bird   will   not   sing,

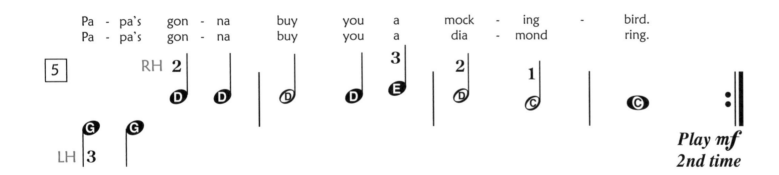

Pa - pa's   gon - na   buy   you   a   mock - ing - bird.
Pa - pa's   gon - na   buy   you   a   dia - mond   ring.

*Play **mf**
2nd time*

Duet: Student plays one octave higher.

Gently

28

New Time Signature

3/4 means 3 counts in every measure.

means a quarter note ♩ gets 1 count.

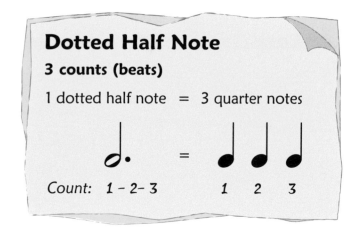

Dotted Half Note

3 counts (beats)

1 dotted half note = 3 quarter notes

♩. = ♩ ♩ ♩

Count: 1 – 2– 3   1 2 3

Rhythm 7

3/4 ♩ ♩ ♩ | ♩.

Count: 1 2 3   1 – 2 – 3

Tap and count aloud 3 times each day.

Let's Take a Trip

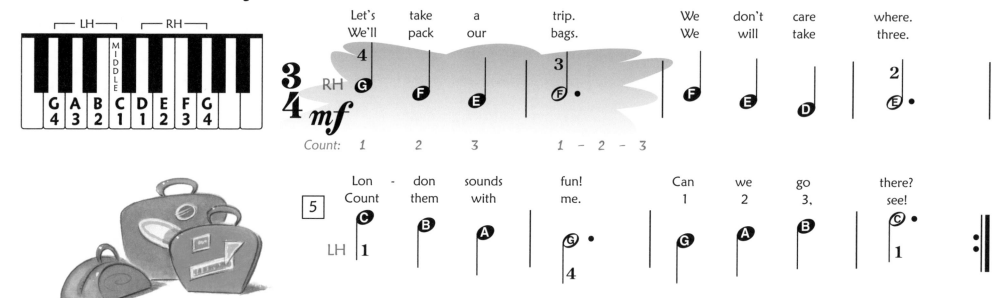

Let's take a trip. We don't care where.
We'll pack our bags. We will take three.

RH: G F E F. F E D E.

Count: 1 2 3 1 – 2 – 3

Lon - don sounds fun! Can we go there?
Count them with me. 1 2 3, see!

LH: C B A G. G A B C.

Closer Look — Circle the steps that move up in *Let's Take a Trip*.
Then, count 1 - 2 - 3 for each measure as you play.

Duet: Student plays one octave higher.

Moderately fast

CD 40/41
GM 21

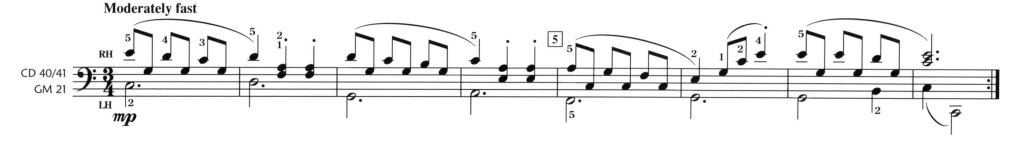

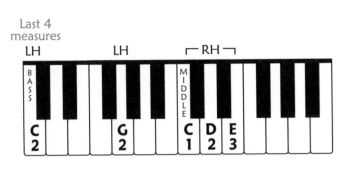

Last 4 measures

Middle C is the C located closest to the middle of the keyboard. Play it with RH 1 and say, "Middle C."

Bass C is one **octave** (8 notes) lower than middle C. Play it with LH 2 and say, "Bass C."

Big Ben

Press the damper pedal and hold throughout.

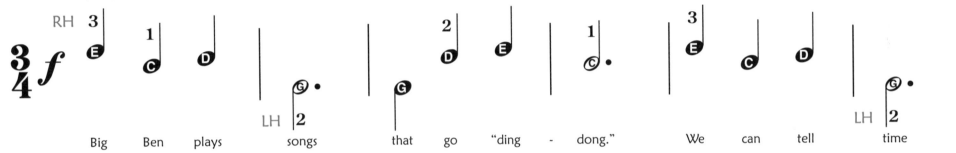

Big Ben plays songs that go "ding - dong." We can tell time

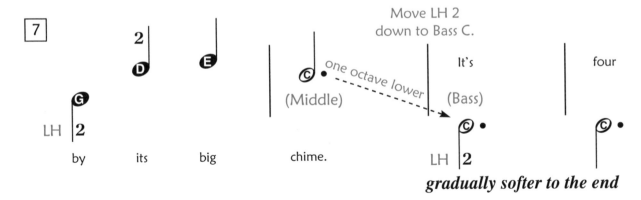

by its big chime. It's four o' - clock.

gradually softer to the end

p

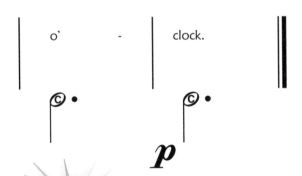

Premier Performer

Play Big Ben again without duet:
- *one octave (8 notes) higher*
- *one octave lower*

Theory Book: page 23
Performance Book: page 12

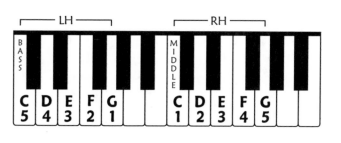

Rhythm 8

3/4 ♩ ♩ ♩.

Count: 1 - 2 - 3   1 - 2 - 3

Tap and count aloud 3 times each day.

Gum Ball Machine

Add finger numbers.

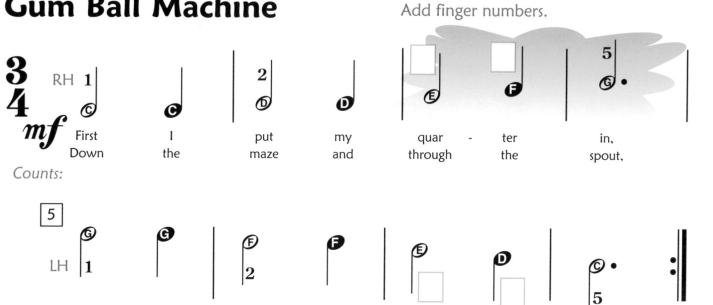

3/4 *mf*

RH 1 C | C | 2 D | D | E | F | 5 G.

First I put my quar - ter in,
Down the maze and through the spout,

Counts:

5

LH 1 G | G | F 2 | F | E | D | C. 5

next the gum ball starts to spin.
then I take my gum ball out.

Counts:

🔍 **Closer Look**   *Write the counts by measure for Gum Ball Machine. Tap and count aloud.*

Duet: Student plays one octave higher.

CD 44/45 GM 23

Happily ... RH ... LH *mp with pedal*

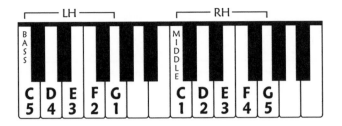

Writing Time

- Draw a continuous line that connects the RH noteheads on the second line of music.

- Notice how the notes step up and down.

Early to Bed

(Words by Benjamin Franklin)

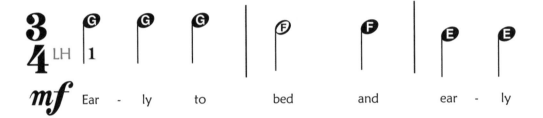

3/4 LH 1 G G G F F E E E D.

mf Ear - ly to bed and ear - ly to rise,

5 RH 2 D E F G F E D E D C.

makes a man health - y and wealth - y and wise.

Imagination Station

Optional ending
without duet:
Move LH 2 down to Bass C and play, repeating several times to chime the hour you wake up. Hold down the damper pedal for the chimes.

Duet: Student plays one octave higher.

Moderately fast

46/47 GM 24

Theory Book: page 24

The Staff

Music is written on the 5 lines and 4 spaces of the **staff.**

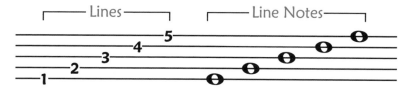

Lines — Line Notes

Spaces — Space Notes

- Point to each line note and say, "line 1, line 2," *etc.*

- Point to each space note and say, "space 1, space 2," *etc.*

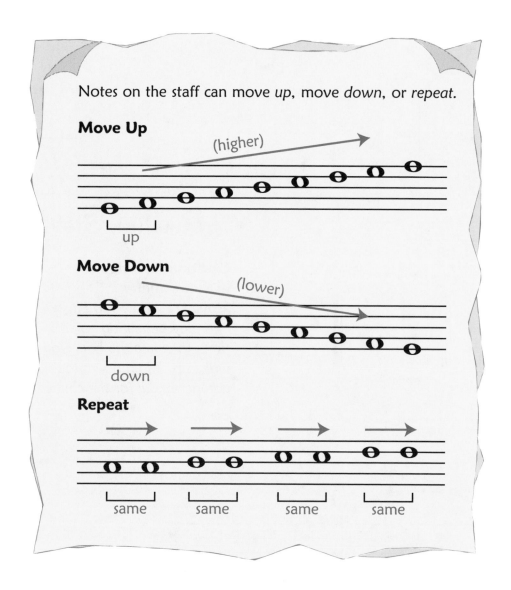

Notes on the staff can move *up*, move *down*, or *repeat.*

Move Up

(higher)

up

Move Down

(lower)

down

Repeat

same   same   same   same

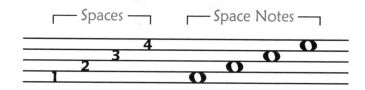

Closer Look

1. Your teacher will play notes and say if they **move up, move down** or **repeat.**

   Teacher: CDEFG; GFEDC; CCCCC

2. Your teacher will play more notes that **move up, move down** or **repeat.** Do the notes move up, move down, or repeat?

   Teacher: *Play five notes in each example.*

Bass Clef   Treble Clef

A **bass clef** on the staff usually shows notes *below* Middle C.

A **treble clef** on the staff usually shows notes *above* Middle C.

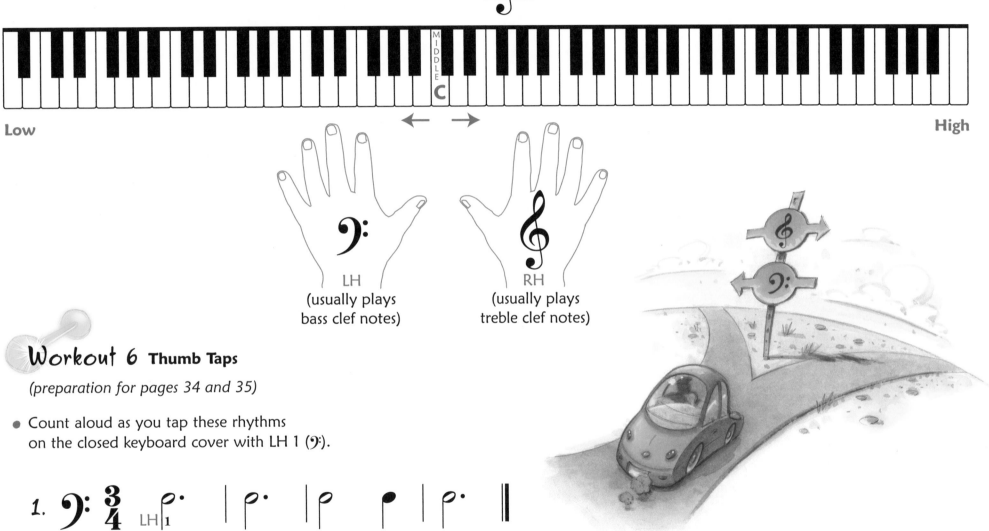

Low   High

LH
(usually plays bass clef notes)

RH
(usually plays treble clef notes)

Workout 6 Thumb Taps

(preparation for pages 34 and 35)

- Count aloud as you tap these rhythms on the closed keyboard cover with LH 1 (𝄢).

1. 𝄢 **3/4** LH 1

2. 𝄢 **4/4** LH 1

- Count and tap the above rhythms again with RH 1 (𝄞).

Theory Book: page 26

Reading Middle C

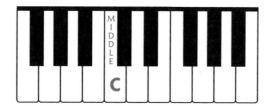

Middle C in Treble Clef

Middle C for RH is written on a short line (ledger line) *below* the treble staff.

Play with RH.

1. f *gradually softer to the end* p

Middle C in Bass Clef

Middle C for LH is written on a short line (ledger line) *above* the bass staff.

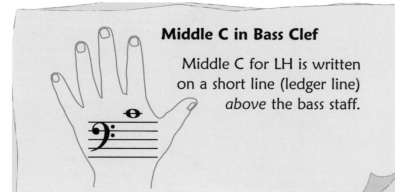

Play with LH.

2. f *gradually softer to the end* p

The Grand Staff

When joined together by a brace, the bass staff and treble staff make the **grand staff.**

Brace →

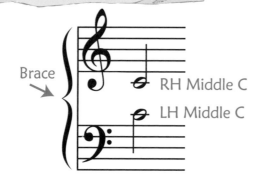

RH Middle C
LH Middle C

On the grand staff, Middle C is written on a ledger line between the treble and bass staffs.

Middle C for RH has a stem that points **up.** It is written closer to the treble staff.

Middle C for LH has a stem that points **down.** It is written closer to the bass staff.

Half Rest

2 counts (beats)

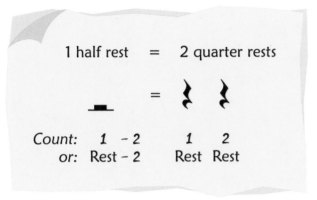

1 half rest = 2 quarter rests

Count: 1 – 2   1   2
or: Rest – 2   Rest Rest

Count: 1 – 2   3 – 4
or: 1 – 2   Rest – 2

Tap and count aloud 3 times each day.

Change on C

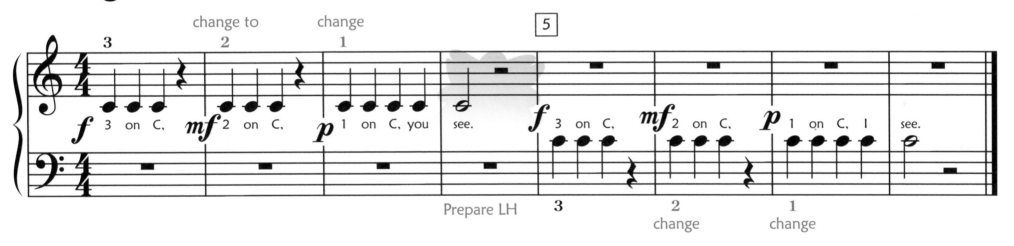

change to   change

3   2   1   5

f 3 on C, **mf** 2 on C, **p** 1 on C, you see.   **f** 3 on C, **mf** 2 on C, **p** 1 on C, I see.

Prepare LH   3   2   1
change   change

Duet: Student plays one octave higher.

Moderately, with a steady beat

CD 48/49 GM 25

RH 3 1   LH 1

mf   **mp**   **pp**

Theory Book: page 28
Performance Book: page 13

Bass F

The bass clef (𝄢) is also called the **F clef.** The F line passes between the two dots.

The note written on the F or 4th line is called **Bass F.** It is *lower* than Middle C.

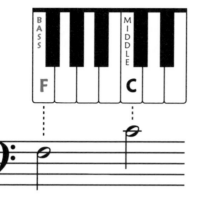

Arrowhead

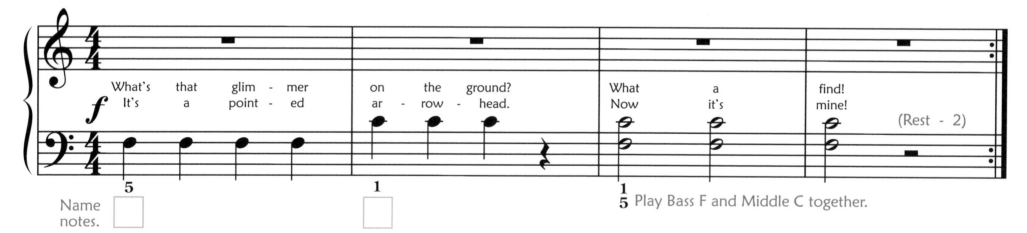

What's that glim - mer on the ground? What a find!
It's a point - ed ar - row - head. Now it's mine!

(Rest - 2)

Name notes.

⁵ Play Bass F and Middle C together.

Duet: Student plays one octave higher.

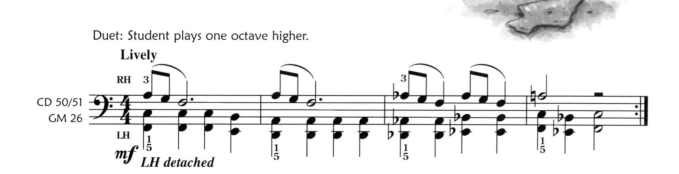

Lively

CD 50/51
GM 26

RH 3

LH ⅕

mf *LH detached*

Premier Performer

Play Arrowhead again without the duet. Press the damper pedal and hold throughout the piece.

Tempo

The speed of the beats in music.

The **tempo marking** is written above the time signature.

My New Piece

Tempo Marking

↘ **Moderately**

Sight-Reading

Play and say the note names as quickly as you can, 3 times each day. Use the correct fingering.

1. *2.* *3.*

2 2 1
      5

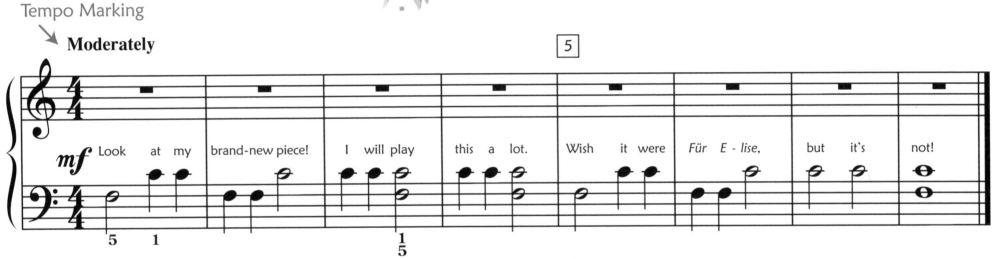

Premier Performer *Keep a rounded hand position when playing My New Piece.*

Adapted from
Ellmenreich's *Spinning Song*

Whole Rest in 3/4

Rest for a whole measure.

In 3/4 time, the whole rest gets 3 counts.

3/4 ▬ ‖

Count: 1 – 2 – 3
or: Rest – 2 – 3

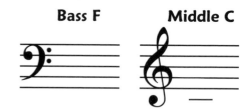

Writing Time

Write the following whole notes:

Bass F   **Middle C**

Waltzing

Moderate waltz tempo

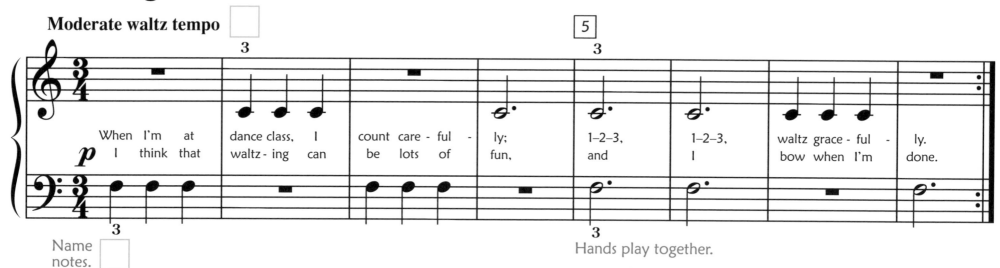

When I'm at / I think that | dance class, I / waltz-ing can | count care-ful- / be lots of | ly; / fun, | 1–2–3, / and | 1–2–3, / I | waltz grace-ful- / bow when I'm | ly. / done.

Name notes.

Hands play together.

Closer Look

Trace the Bass F line in Waltzing *with a red marker or crayon.*

Duet: Student plays one octave higher.

Moderate waltz tempo

CD 54/55
GM 28

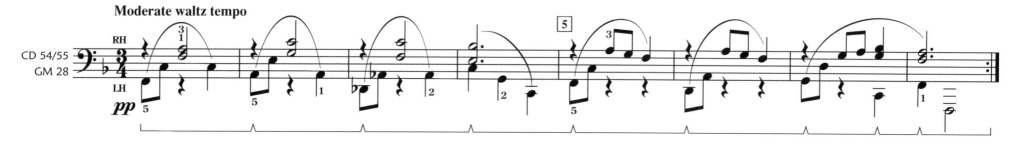

Treble G

The treble clef (𝄞) is also called the **G clef.** It curls around the G line.

The note written on the G line is called **Treble G.** It is *higher* than Middle C.

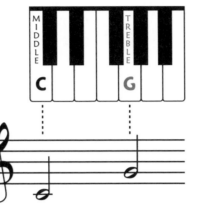

G → Line

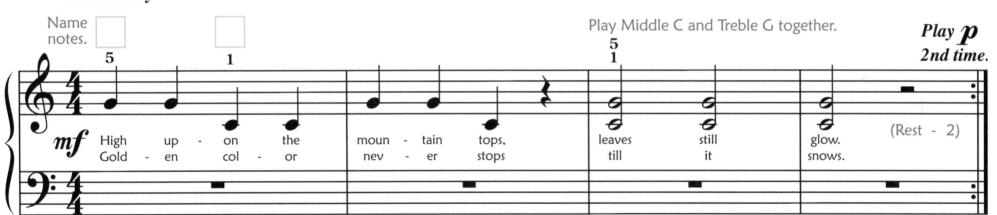

Workout 7 The Tabletop

- Play Middle C and Treble G together with RH 1–5, and hold. The top of your hand and wrist should be level, like a tabletop.

- Now play Middle C and Bass F together with LH 5–1, and hold. Check the "tabletop."

- Practice 3 times each day with RH and LH.

Aspen Trees

Moderately

Name notes.

Play Middle C and Treble G together.

Play *p* 2nd time.

mf

High up - on the
Gold - en col - or

moun - tain tops,
nev - er stops

leaves still
till it

glow.
snows.

(Rest - 2)

Duet: Student plays one octave higher.

Moderately

CD 56/57
GM 29

RH

LH

mp–pp

Premier Performer

Play Aspen Trees again without the duet. Press the damper pedal and hold throughout the piece.

Theory Book: page 31

Ice Pops

Theory Book: page 31

Sight-Reading

Play and say the note names as quickly as you can, 3 times each day. Use the correct fingering.

1.   2   **2.**   2   **3.**   5 / 1

Gently

Name notes. ☐

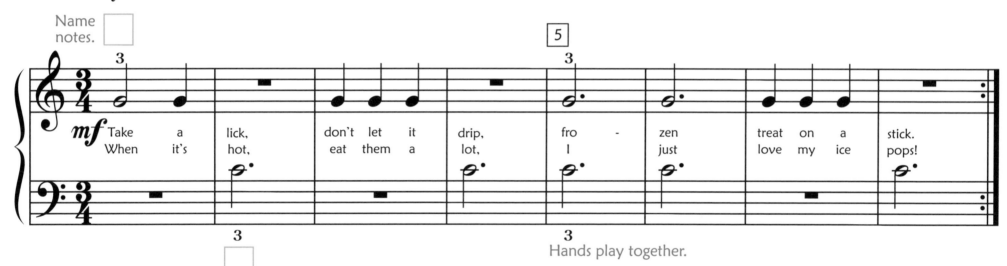

mf

Take a lick, don't let it drip, fro - zen treat on a stick.
When it's hot, eat them a lot, I just love my ice pops!

5

3   3

☐ 3

Hands play together.

Closer Look

Trace the Treble G line in Ice Pops *with a blue marker or crayon.*

Duet: Student plays one octave higher.

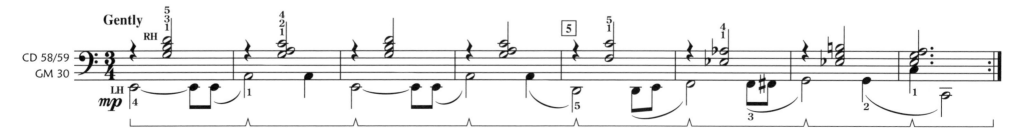

Gently

CD 58/59
GM 30

mp

Landmark Notes

Landmark notes are important
guides to learning other notes.

Treble G

RH Middle C

Bass F

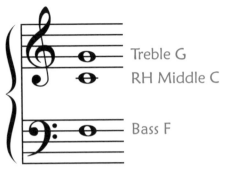

Twinkling Planets

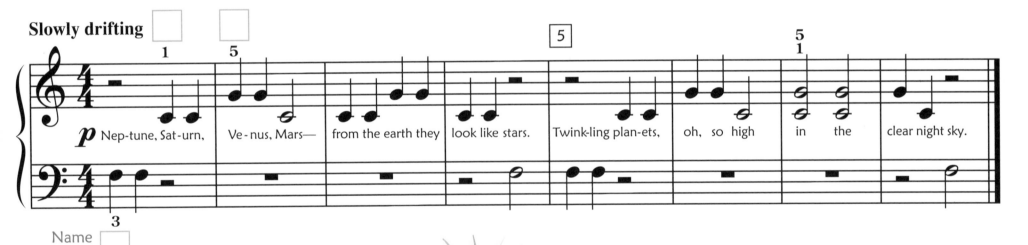

Slowly drifting

Nep-tune, Sat-urn, Ve-nus, Mars— from the earth they look like stars. Twink-ling plan-ets, oh, so high in the clear night sky.

Name
notes.

Premier Performer — *Play* Twinkling Planets *again, without the duet,
high on the keyboard. Press the damper pedal
and hold throughout the piece.*

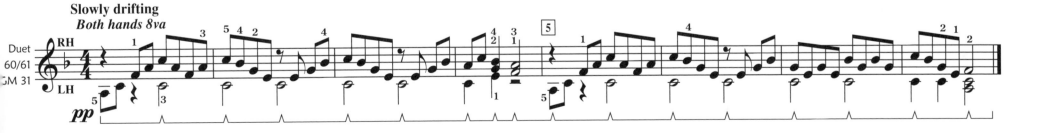

Slowly drifting
Both hands 8va

Duet
60/61
GM 31

RH

LH

pp

Theory Book: page 33

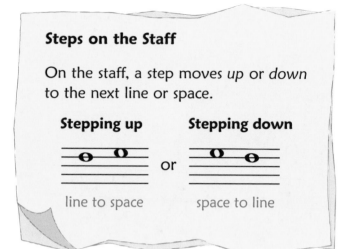

Steps on the Staff

On the staff, a step moves *up* or *down* to the next line or space.

Stepping up   **Stepping down**

or

line to space   space to line

New Note G

a step up from Bass F

Bass G is written in the 4th space of the bass staff.

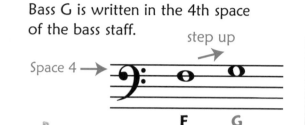

Space 4 →

step up

F   G

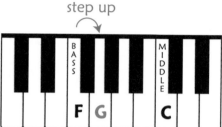

step up

F G   C

Skating

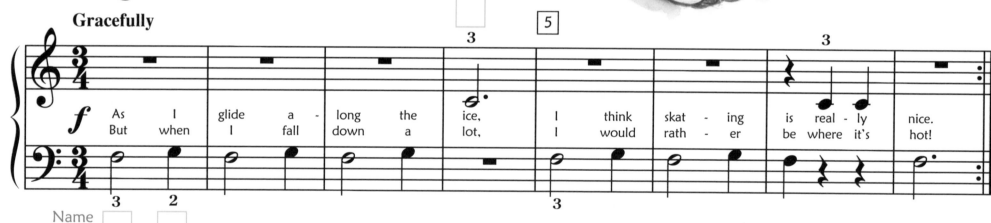

Gracefully

f

As   I   glide   a - long   the   ice,   I   think   skat - ing   is   real - ly   nice.
But   when   I   a   fall   down   the   a   lot,   I   would   rath - er   be   where   it's   hot!

Name notes.   [3]   [2]

Closer Look

Circle each landmark note in Skating.

Duet: Student plays one octave higher.

Gracefully

CD 62/63 GM 32

mf

Theory Book: page 34
Performance Book: page 16

New Note E

a step down from Bass F

Bass E is written in the 3rd space of the bass staff.

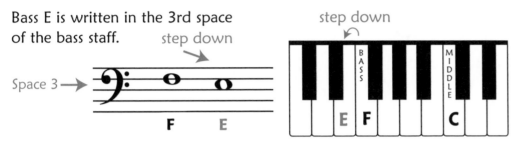

Basketball

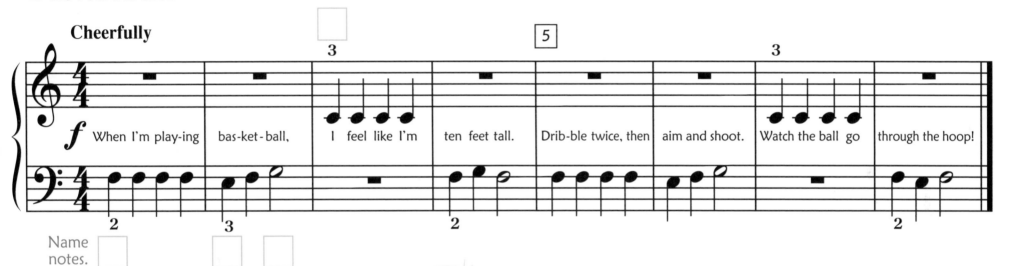

Cheerfully

𝆑 When I'm play-ing | bas-ket-ball, | I feel like I'm | ten feet tall. | Drib-ble twice, then | aim and shoot. | Watch the ball go | through the hoop!

Name notes.

Closer Look Circle each note in Basketball that is **not** a landmark note.
Name the circled notes: _____ and _____

Duet: Student plays one octave higher.

CD 64/65 GM 33

Theory Book: page 35
Performance Book: page 17

New Landmark Note

Bass C is written in the 2nd space of the bass staff.

Bass C is *lower* than Middle C and Bass F.

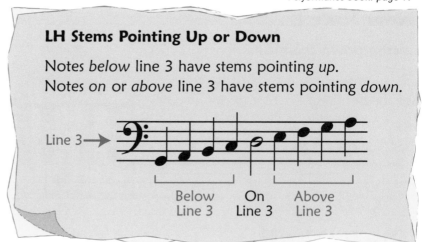

Space 2 →

Bass C   Bass F   LH Middle C

LH Stems Pointing Up or Down

Notes *below* line 3 have stems pointing *up*.
Notes *on* or *above* line 3 have stems pointing *down*.

Line 3 →

Below Line 3   On Line 3   Above Line 3

Trampoline Bounce

Play examples 1 and 2 with your LH.
The LH now plays notes with stems pointing *up* ♩ and *down* ♩

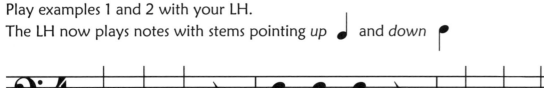

1.

2.

Circle each Bass C.

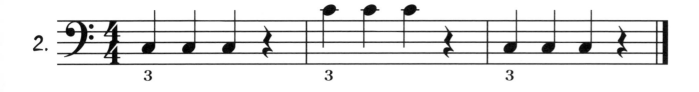

3.

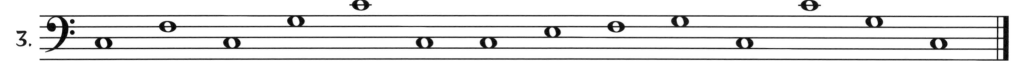

Premier Performer — Name each note in example 3 while playing with LH finger 2.

New Note D
a step up from Bass C

A *step up* from Bass C is D.
A *step up* from D is E.

Starting with Bass C, point to the notes on the staff as you say, "space-line-space, C-D-E."

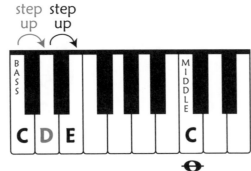

step up · step up

C · D · E
Space · Line · Space
2 · 3 · 3

French Fries

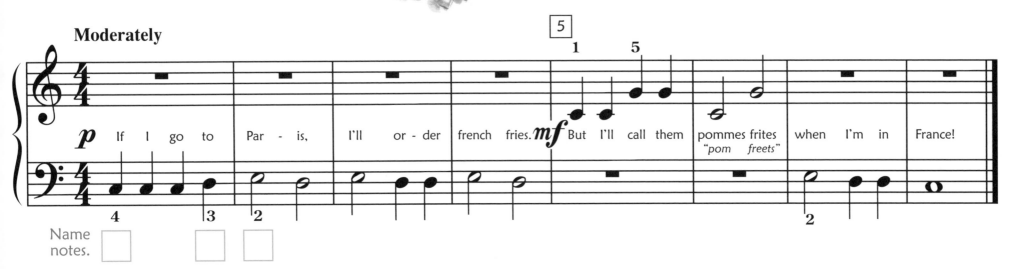

Moderately

p If I go to Par - is, I'll or - der french fries. *mf* But I'll call them pommes frites when I'm in France!
"pom   freets"

Name notes.

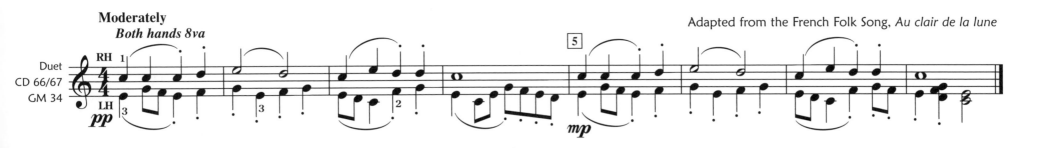

Moderately
Both hands 8va

Adapted from the French Folk Song, *Au clair de la lune*

Duet
CD 66/67
GM 34

Stepping Up from Bass C

for the C 5-finger pattern

Bass C and the four notes that step up from it are called the *C 5-finger pattern*.

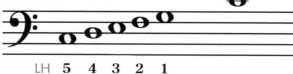

LH 5 4 3 2 1

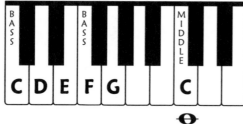

Workout 8 5-Finger Checklist for LH

As you play *Skateboard Champ*, check the following:

- Do your hand and wrist make a tabletop?
- Are you playing on the fingertip pads of fingers 5, 4, 3 and 2?
- Are you playing on the side tip of the thumb?

Skateboard Champ

With confidence

Let's go to the | skate-board park; | I wish we could | stay till dark. | Rid-ing up and | down the ramps, | I feel like a | skate-board champ.

mf 5 — stepping up — 1 | 1 — stepping down — 5 | *f*

Premier Performer

Play Skateboard Champ *again one octave higher with RH. Begin on Middle C with finger 1. Then play hands together.*

Duet: Student plays **two** octaves higher.

CD 68/69 GM 35

Johann Sebastian Bach (1685–1750), born in Germany, is one of the most famous composers of all time. He wrote several minuets for his 20 children (four of whom also became composers). These pieces are still popular with piano students today.

Sight-Reading

Play and say the note names as quickly as you can, 3 times each day. Use the correct fingering.

1.   2.   3.
2   1   3

Minuet for Bach

Thoughtfully

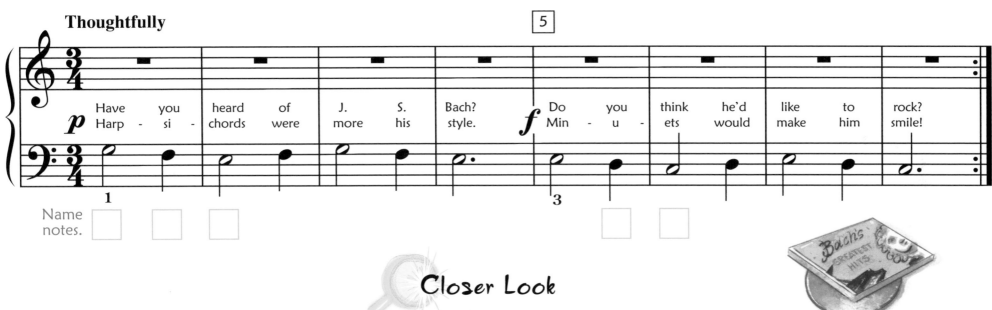

Have you heard of J. S. Bach? Do you think he'd like to rock?
Harp - si - chords were more his style. Min - u - ets would make him smile!

Name notes.

Closer Look

Circle each landmark note in Minuet for Bach.

Adapted from Bach's *Minuet in G Major*

Thoughtfully

Duet
CD 70/71 GM 36

Theory Book: page 38

New Notes D and E

step up from Middle C

A *step up* from Middle C is D.
A *step up* from D is E.

Starting with Middle C, point to the notes on the staff as you say, "line-space-line, C-D-E."

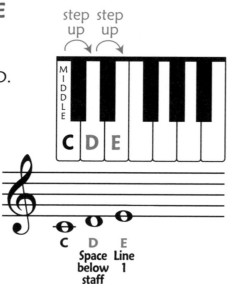

step step
up up

C D E

C D E
Space Line
below 1
staff

Rhythm 10

Count: 1 - 2 - 3   4

Tap and count aloud 3 times each day.

Alouette

Moderately   Name notes.

5

mf   A - lou - et - te,   gen- tille a - lou - et - te,   a - lou - et - te,   je te plu - me - rai.

2

Premier Performer   *Play* Alouette *again, starting with RH 1 on C.*

Adapted from Clementi's Sonatina in C Major, *Op. 36, No. 1*

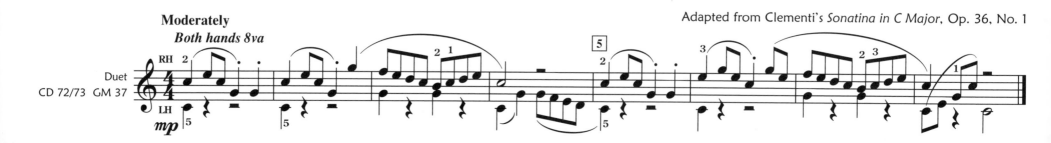

Moderately
Both hands 8va

Duet
CD 72/73 GM 37

RH 2

LH

mp 5

New Note F

a step down from Treble G

Treble F is written in the
1st space of the treble staff.

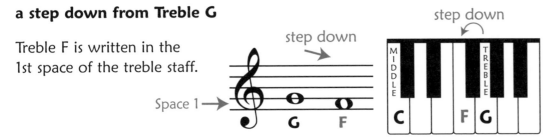

My Kite

Smoothly

Name notes. ☐ ☐

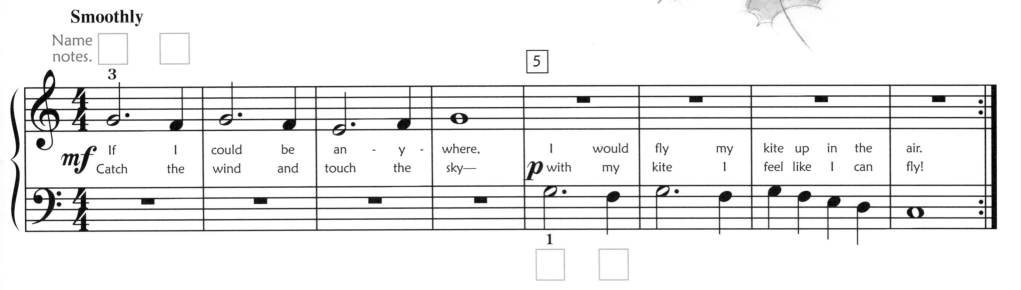

mf If I could be an-y- where, I would fly my kite up in the air.
Catch the wind and touch the sky— *p* with my kite I feel like I can fly!

🔍 **Closer Look** *Trace the Treble G line in My Kite with a **blue** marker or crayon. Trace the Bass F line with a **red** marker or crayon.*

Duet: Student plays **two** octaves higher.

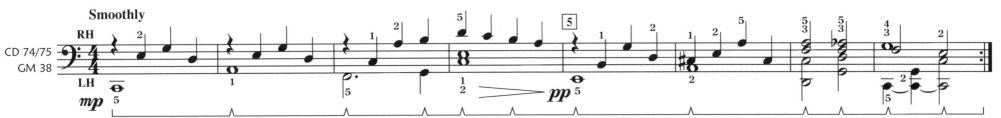

Theory Book: page 40

Stepping Up from Middle C

for the C 5-finger pattern

Middle C and the four notes that step up from it are called the *C 5-finger pattern.*

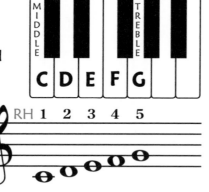

Workout 9 **5-Finger Checklist for RH**

As you play *All-Star Game,* check the following:

● Do your hand and wrist make a tabletop?

● Are you playing on the fingertip pads of fingers 2, 3, 4 and 5?

● Are you playing on the side tip of the thumb?

All-Star Game

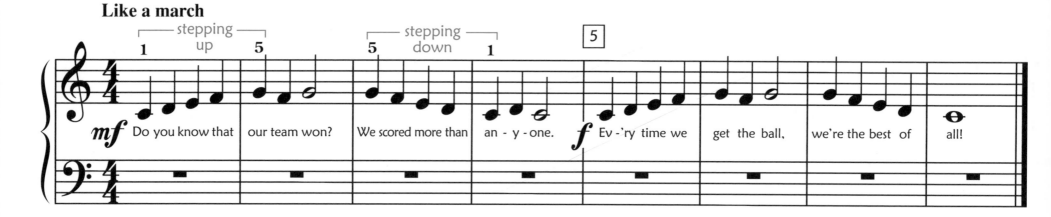

Like a march

stepping up
stepping down

mf Do you know that | our team won? | We scored more than | an-y-one. *f* Ev-'ry time we | get the ball, | we're the best of | all!

Premier Performer Play All-Star Game *again one octave lower with LH. Begin on Bass C with finger 5. Then play hands together.*

Duet: Student plays one octave higher.

Like a march

CD 76/77
GM 39

mp *mf*

Ludwig van Beethoven *(1770–1827), born in Bonn, Germany, composed some of the greatest music ever written. Even though he lost his hearing later in life, he continued to write great masterpieces, including the popular* Ode to Joy *from his* Ninth Symphony.

Sight-Reading

Play and say the note names as quickly as you can, 3 times each day. Use the correct fingering.

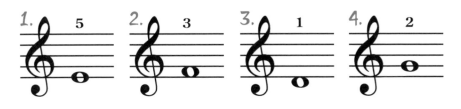

Ode to Joy

(*Theme from the* Ninth Symphony)

Ludwig van Beethoven

Steady and strong

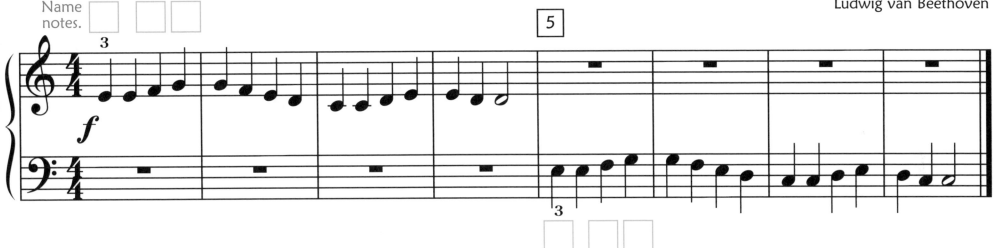

Closer Look *Circle each landmark note in* Ode to Joy.

Duet: Student plays one octave higher.

Steady and strong

CD 78/79
GM 40

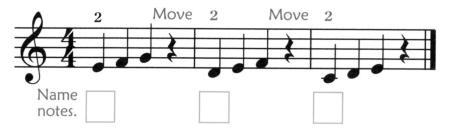

Workout 10 **On the Move**

The hand can move so the same finger can play different notes.
Use this workout to prepare for the RH of *A Page or Two*.

Name notes. ☐ ☐ ☐

Practice 3 times each day.

A Page or Two

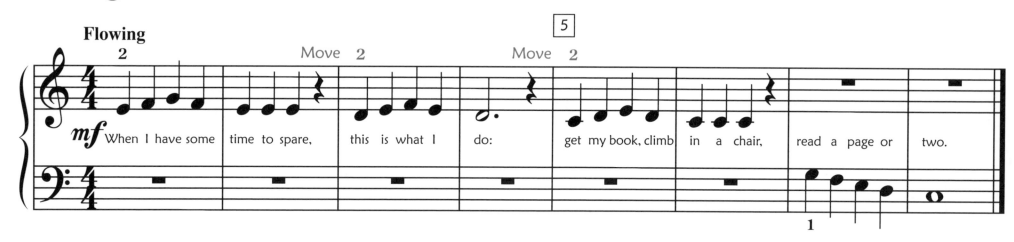

Flowing

mf When I have some time to spare, this is what I do: get my book, climb in a chair, read a page or two.

Premier Performer *Play* A Page or Two *again, using finger 1 in the RH instead of finger 2.*

Duet: Student plays **two** octaves higher.

CD 80/81 GM 41

New Notes B and A

step down from Middle C

A *step down* from Middle C is B.
A *step down* from B is A.

Starting with Middle C,
point to the notes on
the staff as you say,
"line-space-line, C-B-A."

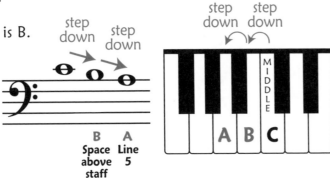

Rhythm Review

On your lap, tap each rhythm 3 times daily as
you count aloud.

Snowy Day

Moderate waltz tempo

mf Skies full of snow, winds that are cold, f we want to go out-side, but Mom says no.
In - side we'll stay, stuck here all day. We wish the snow would stop so we can play.

Name notes.

Duet: Student plays one octave higher.

Moderate waltz tempo

CD 82/83 GM 42

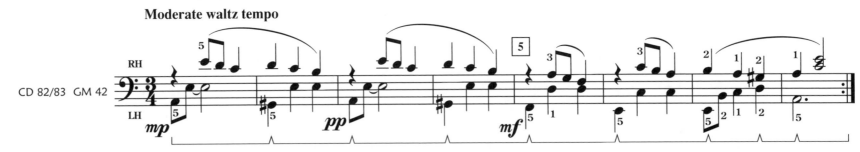

Theory Book: page 43
Performance Book: page 24

Stepping Down from Middle C

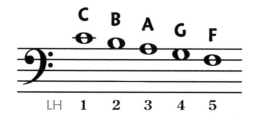

C B A G F
LH 1 2 3 4 5

Sight-Reading

Play and say the note names as quickly as you can, 3 times each day. Use the correct fingering.

1.   *2.*   *3.*

2   2   1

Bike Ride

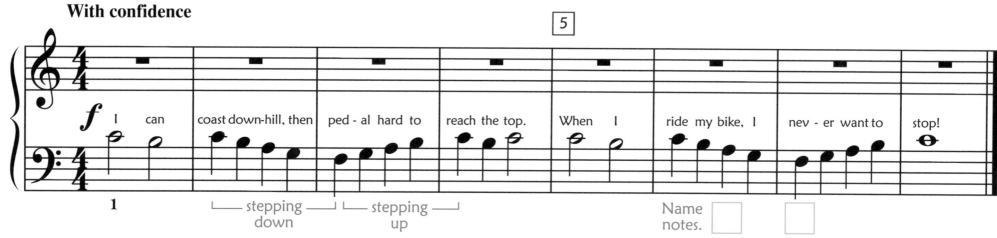

With confidence

5

f | I | can | coast down-hill, then | ped - al hard to | reach the top. | When | I | ride my bike, I | nev - er want to | stop!

1

stepping down   stepping up

Name notes. ☐ ☐

Duet: Student plays one octave higher.

With confidence

CD 84/85 GM 43

RH LH *mf*

Premier Performer Play Bike Ride *again with RH, starting with finger 5. Play softly and slowly.*

Rhythm Review

1. 4/4

2. 4/4

On your lap, tap each rhythm 3 times daily as you count aloud.

Old Joe Clark

Lively

Name note.

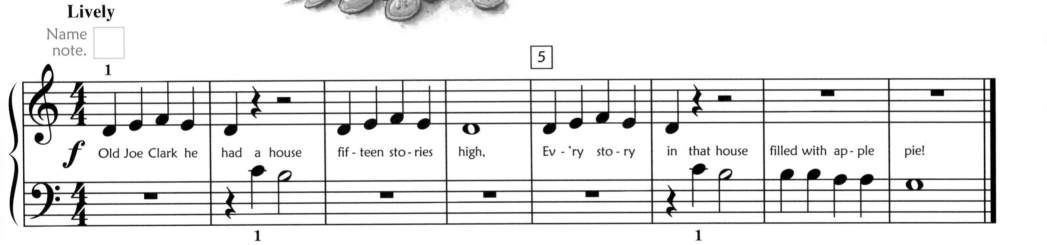

Old Joe Clark he had a house fif-teen sto-ries high, Ev-'ry sto-ry in that house filled with ap-ple pie!

Duet: Student plays one octave higher.

Lively

CD 86/87 GM 44

Theory Book: page 44
Performance Book: page 25

Skip

A skip moves *up* or *down*:
- skipping a white key
- skipping a finger
- skipping a letter

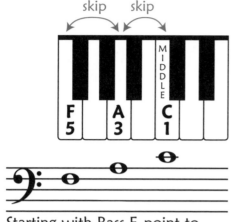

Starting with Bass F, point to the notes on the staff as you say, "line-line-line, F–A–C."

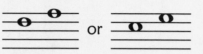 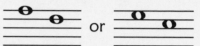

Skips on the Staff

On the staff, a skip moves *up* or *down*, line to line or space to space.

Skipping up

or

line to line   space to space

Skipping down

or

line to line   space to space

Hopscotch

With a steady beat

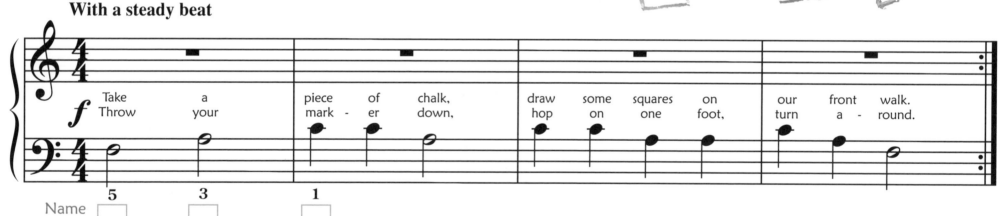

Take   a   piece   of   chalk,   draw   some   squares   on   our   front   walk.
Throw   your   mark - er   down,   hop   on   one   foot,   turn   a - round.

Name notes.   5   3   1

Closer Look Point to each skip in Hopscotch *and say "skip up"
or "skip down." Then name each note aloud.*

Duet: Student plays one octave higher.

With a steady beat

CD 88/89 GM 45

Skip Up from Middle C

A *skip up* from Middle C is E.
A *skip up* from E is G.

Starting with Middle C, point to the notes on the staff as you say, "line-line-line, C–E–G."

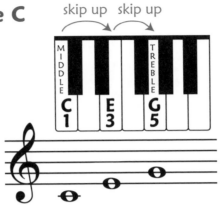

Rise and Shine!

Rhythm Review

On your lap, tap each rhythm 3 times daily as you count aloud.

March tempo (bugle call)

Name notes.

mf

| When | it's | six | o' - clock, | Mom | comes | in, | but | does - | n't | knock. |
| She | says, | "Rise | and | shine!" | But | I | hope | she'll | change | her | mind! |

Closer Look *Point to each skip in* Rise and Shine! *and say, "skip up" or "skip down." Then name each note aloud.*

Duet: Student plays one octave higher.

Adapted from the bugle call, *Reveille*

March tempo (bugle call)

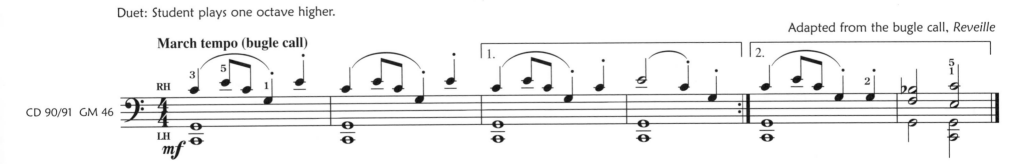

CD 90/91 GM 46

mf

58

Skip Up from D

A *skip up* from D is F.

Starting with D, point to the notes on the staff as you say, "space-space, D-F."

Rhythm Review

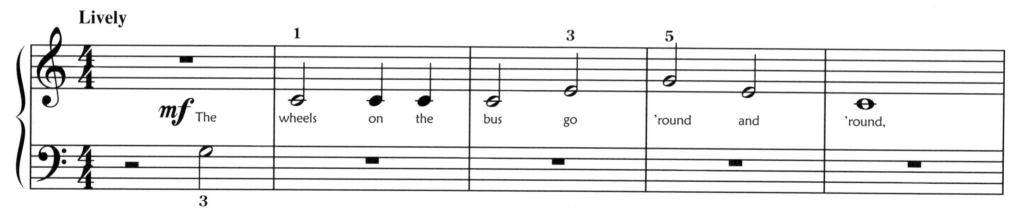

On your lap, tap each rhythm 3 times daily as you count aloud.

The Wheels on the Bus

Lively

mf The wheels on the bus go 'round and 'round,

Count: 1 - 2   3 - 4

Duet: Student plays one octave higher.

Lively

CD 92/93 GM 47

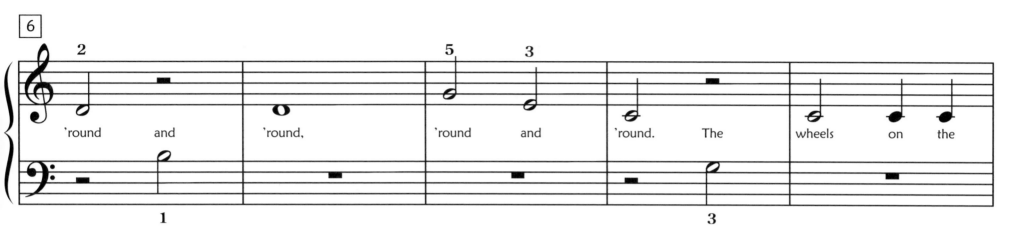

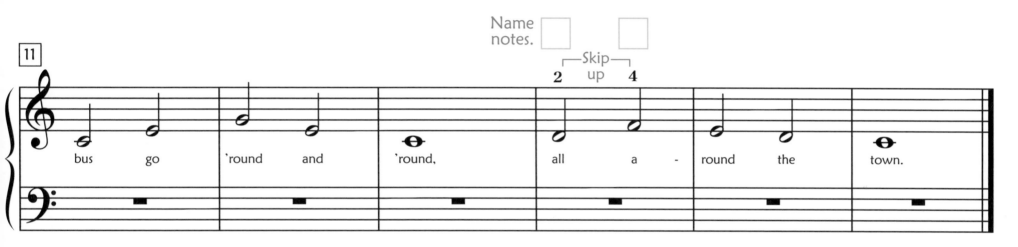

Name notes. ☐ ☐

Closer Look

Circle each landmark note in
The Wheels on the Bus.

Wolfgang Amadeus Mozart *(1756–1791), a musical genius, was born in Salzburg, Austria. His father began teaching him piano when he was only four years old. Mozart wrote Eine Kleine Nachtmusik (A Little Night Music) for orchestra in 1787.*

Sight-Reading

Play and say the note names as quickly as you can, 3 times each day. Use the correct fingering.

Eine Kleine Mozart

(Theme from Eine Kleine Nachtmusik)

Wolfgang Amadeus Mozart

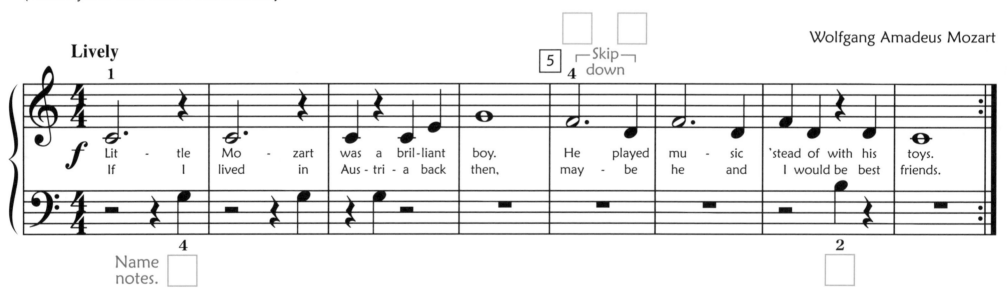

Duet: Student plays one octave higher.

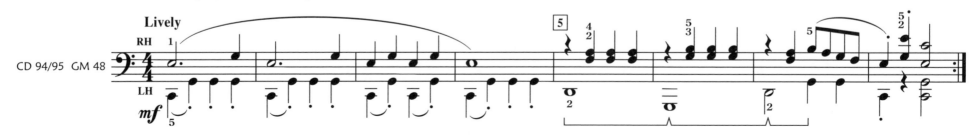

CD 94/95 GM 48

Skip Down from B

A *skip down* from B is G.

Starting with B, point to the notes on the staff as you say, "space-space, B-G."

skip down

B G

skip down

MIDDLE

G B

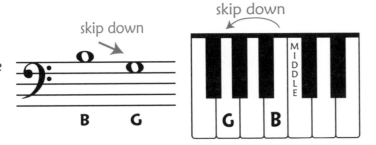

Franz Joseph Haydn *(1732–1809) is known as the father of the symphony. In Surprise Symphony, Haydn used sudden loud sounds as a musical joke—supposedly to wake members of the audience who had fallen asleep. Haydn and Mozart, both from Austria, were friends and admired each other's music.*

Haydn's Surprise

(Theme from Surprise Symphony)

Franz Joseph Haydn

Moderately

mf What would Hay-dn | say to us? | Would he find it | cur - i - ous? *p* If we had him | close his eyes, *f* and we shout-ed | out, "Sur-prise!"

Name notes. 1 3

🪐 **Imagination Station**

The melody for the duet on page 57 contains many skips. Your teacher will show you how to play it.

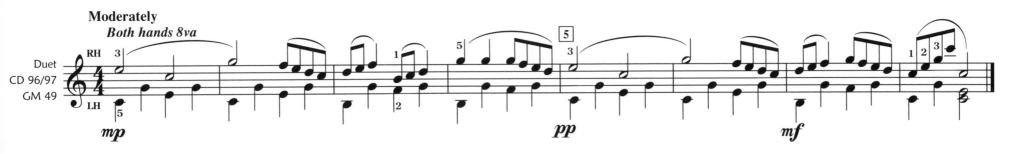

Moderately
Both hands 8va

Duet
CD 96/97
GM 49

mp   *pp*   *mf*

Theory Book: page 48
Performance Book: pages 30–31

Performance Tips

It is fun and challenging to play pieces you know for friends and family. Here are some performance tips:

- Before starting, think about the tempo and dynamics of the first measures.

- After you begin, keep going—no matter what!

- After you finish, put your hands on your lap.

- Stand to face the audience and bow slowly.

- Smile and feel proud of what you've accomplished!

Time to Celebrate

With confidence

Time to cel - e - brate and smile; all my work has been worth-while. Now it's time to

Premier Performer   *Play* Time to Celebrate *for a family member or friend. Remember the Performance Tips.*

Duet: Student plays one octave higher.

With confidence

CD 98/99
GM 50

mf
marcato

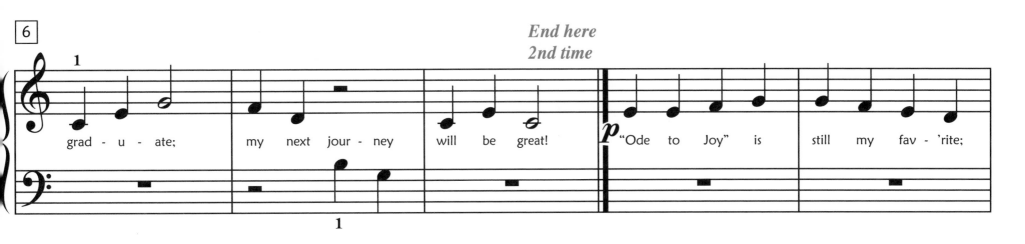

End here
2nd time

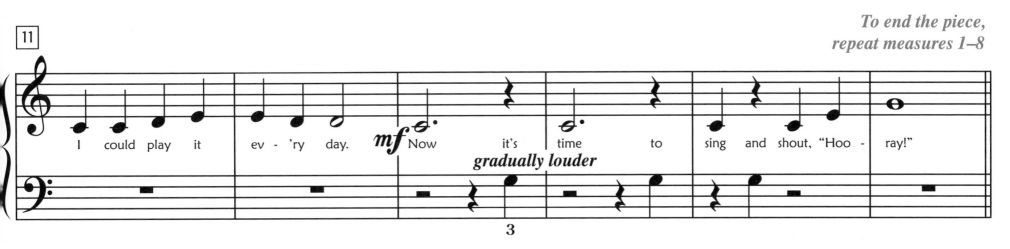

To end the piece,
repeat measures 1–8

Alfred's

Premier Performer
Piano Achievement Award

presented to

_____
Student

You have

successfully completed

Lesson Book 1A

and are

hereby promoted to

Lesson Book 1B.

_____
Teacher

_____
Date